Lose to Find

poems by

Steve Wilson

Finishing Line Press
Georgetown, Kentucky

Lose to Find

Copyright © 2018 by Steve Wilson
ISBN 978-1-63534-554-4 First Edition
All rights reserved under International and Pan-American Copyright Conventions. No part of this book may be reproduced in any manner whatsoever without written permission from the publisher, except in the case of brief quotations embodied in critical articles and reviews.

ACKNOWLEDGMENTS

A number of poems in this collection, some in previous versions, appeared in the following journals and websites: *Beloit Poetry Journal, Cimarron Review,* the "Ekphrastic Poetry" online feature of the Maier Museum of Art at Randolph College, *Midwest Quarterly, New American Writing, Rio Grande Review, San Pedro River Review, Texas Observer,* and *Two Hawks Quarterly.*

Publisher: Leah Maines
Editor: Christen Kincaid
Cover Art: Debangana Banerjee
Author Photo: Connor Wilson
Cover Design: Elizabeth Maines McCleavy

Printed in the USA on acid-free paper.
Order online: www.finishinglinepress.com
also available on amazon.com

Author inquiries and mail orders:
Finishing Line Press
P. O. Box 1626
Georgetown, Kentucky 40324
U. S. A.

Table of Contents

A Weekday 1
Six Storms 2
Unbuilt 3
Green Ruins 4
Resistance 5
Cells: did you make it home 6
Cells: Evening 7
Cells: moon tonight 8
A Sunset 9
Buffalo Bayou 10
Abstracts 11
New Mexico Haiku 12
The Light on the Last Day 13
Lament for A_____. 14
Hours: hinges 15
Violently sundered 16
A Couple 17
On Texas, 2016 18
3 AM Meditation 19
Of April 20
The Real Itself 21
Hida 23
Within Some Globe of Sleep 24
Coumeenole Beach 25
Call it a kind of grace 26
Righteousness 27
In My Dreams I Am Whole 28

A Weekday

                    —above
the power lines, the

           crosswalk,
                    a hundred or more

                waxwings
           break toward

cedar elms and
                the river,

                              lunch-hour faces
  opening to dark

wings on the air
                       astir—

Six Storms

Storms flower, the skies
blackening to slate. Nightjars
dive into an echo.

***

Rain thunders in, all teeth and bone.

***

Autumn storms conjure
a second spring—
fall greens, blooms,
in spite of itself.

***

Under lowering skies, summer
growls and glowers, then goes.

***

—the eloquence of mist at storm's edge—

***

storms
descended—evening
all day

Unbuilt

: for words are
bodies are words for :

    ***

/ lamp, hat rack—seconds
still, a becalmed lake—
cabinet, mantel, hinge /

    ***

Urge is an itch, a stitch, a helve.
An itch, a stitch—a swerve
we could work our wants through.

    ***

—simplicities, unutterable
as shades, approach—

    ***

Untethered,
full of mind: ghosts
moving
through smoke.

Green Ruins

Up late investigating
versions. You,
or you as you.

      ***

Find me wandering
in the thread-bare hours.

      ***

So much of what is,
is past. A confusion—
back trail—of tangled branches.

      ***

Sight lines—I
to they, know to be,
drift to need.

      ***

I see the world I cannot—see—
the shroud's—faint intimations

      ***

First fruits—
new leaves on the path,
these few words.

Resistance
    —*San Marcos, Nov. 2016*

        Within morning's unsettled light,

  students stride out
into the streets,

      shocked by
        their hopefulness,

  the dark wine

      of their defiance—

            comrades, gathering
         to breach the battlements.

Cells: did you make it home

I texted *did you make it home?*

And then I texted *nothing but snow all day.*
And then *the lowering light, the harbor.*
And I texted *sometimes just watching*

the water is enough, the gulls
and their insistences. **I texted** *the door is*
still open. **I texted** *tree roots, your driveway*

noons. you thought about leaving
before you left. **I texted** *who said*
time and tide? who imagined?

Then *so many days of snow.*

                         You texted *the roads were terrible.*

                    And then you texted *ice. ice and ice.*
                       And then *you and your coastlines.*
                            And you texted *sound does it*

                                  for me. waves. the bell far out
                    beyond the lights. **You texted** *we've been*
                            over this. **You texted** *whatever*

                            home was. I made it out of that
                         empty space. **You texted** *no poems.*
                               not this time, ok? not now.

                                         Then *ice*

Cells: Evening

I texted *the deliciousness of endings.*

And then I texted *work done and sunlight.*
And then *endings made me want to see you.*
And I texted *I could have come with you*

if you had waited an hour. the two of us
*then, and the autumn elm*s. **I texted** *a long way,*
that path. **I texted** *levees, windscreens,*

walls of glass I walk into, shifts
of scene. **I texted** *comfort*
at the end of a long day. that's all.

Then *not much to ask.*

                    You texted *I'm down in the canyon now.*

                    And then you texted *walking, walking.*
          And then *within my own spaces, paths, shades.*
                            And you texted *alone*

                      and myself for this little while,
                       outside you. **You texted** *borders*
                 I'm tending. **You texted** *they grant me*

                        shards of my self, cracks
                   for breath. **You texted** *exactly,*
                   exactly, exactly. my own ways.

                                 Then *for you.*

Cells: moon tonight

I **texted** *moon tonight*

And then I texted *everything silvery blue.*
And then *blue like there's no end.*
And I texted *a long cascading*

*of light lovers could love
inside.* **I texted** *can you
see your way back?* **I texted** *so sure*

*we've been in our silences,
our arrangements.* **I texted** *meet me
at the schoolyard, like before.*

Then *bring your old desires.*

                                         You texted *behind the trees.*

                      And then you texted *a strange light, yes.*
                            And then *always the romantic.*
                                And you texted *wandering off*

                                      *someplace dreams made,
                        under moonglow.* **You texted** *under
moonglow and want.* **You texted** *years*

                                *make us comfortable, I guess,
                                and wary.* **You texted** *the field
                                  near the road to the river.*

                                                Then *i remember.*

A Sunset

                                        —blossoming within

              the wild

ambitions of their laughter,
      children at play

                    beneath the sudden stars—

Buffalo Bayou
   —August 2017

                        the ground
                  undone by flood,

         floats an ocean
     of silences

         and glass—
                                    downtown,

                              ghost roads
                               navigate

         the dirt-browned,
             deepening waters

Abstracts

                      Look, ok, whatever is
            beyond the body is

                precipitous—abysmal, a cliff over:
                notions
                that diffuse and diffuse
                above the roiling Atlantic,

      that tree-to-tree even
the merest of warblers
            dart through. Look,

      it's not so much the unknown
                    as the unmade—its sprawl

                          and everywhere-ness.

There's hurt in here,

      at least. Ache.
Ache's shape.

New Mexico Haiku
—after Adams' "Aspens, Northern New Mexico"

        aspens

                at nightfall—white

fissures of

                light—
                  fade
             to shadow:

            thought

       hushed within

          distance

The Light on the Last Day
—Gougane Barra, Ireland

    What color
          the light
             on the last day? Steel,

              like moon
       sparking
           upon the lake.

From inside shadow,
           the sobered green of dawn,
   of forests.

          Gray suggestions, huddled
along the path. Brown of
             fernroot. Or sky,

now loosing the sun's frayed white
        edges, still purpled dark
    with mountains and night.

Lament for A_____

                      Like ragged cliffs
                            above the surge,

          like the fraying edges

   of ourselves:
              breaking, we are
              broken things,

                          unable

              to speak—

  wary now within

                the afternoon's light, blue

                        and fracturing.

Hours: hinges

By the lowed light of the storm—
dusk at midday—I meet myself
in old poems. I'd forgotten him.
Where did this mind go?

**

Merely to speak—an act of collaboration.
Reverence, and its breath, together
against a deep, darkening dream.

**

Entranced again by that old trauma,
its distortions. They shift and tremor
at the edge of stillness: moiré,
phantasmagoria, mirror ball.

**

Hours: hinges, by which we read
now left now right, beyond
the hills and back before,
to shape our unsaid selves.

**

At the center—only this,
enough—a white sky
and the rain, a gray road.

Violently sundered

                                         Violently sundered,

                            shattered, we are

            ash

                        and debris—

     ragged
     fragments

           of song now

                     borne away
          by the light.

A Couple

—before we were—
we slept within

our own small moments—
not looking for—not
thinking toward—

certain selves—content—
contained—silver pools
of thought that sparked

sometimes on wind
and words and light—

On Texas, 2016

                        Hoping for something

    still open, for openness,

we follow that long highway

            west   (parched scrubs,

double-wides beside

the bonedry creeks,

            the sprawling

red mesas outside Ozona).

At Sanderson,

                everything bolted down

      tight.   Closed faces.

3 AM Meditation

—ghost, river
of motion,
I am

drowned,
downed
enough

to let it go,
go dark:
its syllables

of loss,
long roads
winding out—

Of April
—after Audubon's "Marsh Wren"

                like light
           down a canyon,

like treefall,

        thought

    opens itself

    on spring—

         marsh wrens

                  chittering
        from the rushes

The Real Itself

—a long walk through
        this gray morning. sounds
take shape—

    ***

Maybe it's a whirr,
or a word, out there. A whirr,
a word, perhaps, that stirs
the air's hypnotic calms.

    ***

Every moment sparks
fugitive, elusive: a fox,
darting through the hedgerows.

    ***

Not words alone. Not dreams,
not harm, hurt. The real itself
floats indistinct
upon the light-fraught sky.

    ***

The footpath as it ravels
along the night's edges. I would follow
my own illuminations.

***

Sun flames violet
above the canyonlands—
the poem *en plein air*.

Hida

For Israa, Baghdad

                    Do you,
            alone
                      in your thoughts,
                              wander out sometimes

into such silences?
        A sky
    alive with dark

                birds; rain
        on city streets, troubled
        by the afternoon.

I am
with you. I am

                      with you there—

            a faint reflection
            in the deep
                    well

                      of your self.

Within Some Globe of Sleep

                    Within
some globe of sleep the night
    conjures: valleys

            the mind turns;

                  shapes for /
               patterns of, want

                and taste   and reach—
                from within

                          sleep's hollows,
     calls forth
        hesitant birds,

    their song.

Coumeenole Beach
—Slea Head Grotto, Ireland. August, 2010

From hurt the heart unwords itself.
Goes down to dark. Sits silent.

No breaks, I'd thought, were working
there. Then roar. Then seafoam blast:

a wound was waiting. Feeds to grow.
Now alters, rends. That one long strand,

like faith, curves out uncalmed, thinned
to a breath—just so at once I'm done,

I'm lost. Yes, white the waves that scar
the shore. Yes, cold the roiling deep.

Call it a kind of grace

                      if, as
     summer

                            heat blossoms

                          to flame
    on the mesa,

    cardinals—
                their
      scarlet

                      coruscating against sun-

   light—within the withered
brushwood

      settle and show

Righteousness
    (Orlando)

                    Tell me, then, where is the sin
    in touching, being
        touched by,

                in needing, when
            down the dark streets
                    people scatter, dazed

      and hiding, hurt,
            calling from
        the shadows again?

In My Dreams I Am Whole

In my dreams I am whole
and ready, heading out—eagerness
in the air itself. Even at stop signs
all motion and movement.

In my dreams a dark green
that is like river, water—it goes,
flows now out toward the hollows
and I go too, I follow, I agree, I do.

In my dreams you and I, out early
in a gray boat—the lake blossoms
broad and silvering, light easing over
the treeline—and the shore, the shore.
        There are miles yet to the shore.

Steve Wilson has published hundreds of poems in journals such as *Beloit Poetry Journal, Borderlands, Bluestem, Rio Grande Review, Cimarron Review, Commonweal, Poem, Georgetown Review, North American Review, America, The Christian Science Monitor, Blue Unicorn, New Orleans Review, San Pedro River Review, The Christian Century, New American Writing, Isotope: A Journal of Literary Nature and Science Writing, Midwest Quarterly, The Rio Grande Review,* and *New Letters*; as well as in a number of anthologies, including *O Taste and See: Food Poems* (Bottom Dog Press), *Visiting Frost: Poems Inspired by Robert Frost* (University of Iowa), *Stories from Where We Live: The Gulf Coast* (Milkweed Editions), *Like Thunder: Poets Respond to Violence in America* (University of Iowa), *What Have You Lost?* (Greenwillow), *American Diaspora: Poetry of Displacement* (University of Iowa), *An Introduction to the Prose Poem* (Firewheel Editions), *Beloved on the Earth: 150 Poems of Grief and Gratitude* (Holy Cow! Press), *Classifieds: An Anthology of Prose Poems* (Equinox), *Improbable Worlds: An Anthology of Texas and Louisiana Poets* (Mutabilis) and *Going Down Grand: Poetry of the Grand Canyon* (Lithic). He is the author of three poetry collections: *Allegory Dance, The Singapore Express,* and *The Lost Seventh*; and editor of *The Anatomy of Water: A Sampling of Contemporary American Prose Poetry.* He lives in San Marcos, Texas.